Copyright © 2013
By Ged Austin

All rights reserved.

The right of Ged Austin to be identified as the author of this work has been asserted by him in accordance with the copyright, Designs and Patents Act, 1998.

Publishing history

First Edition April 2013

Email: jediaustin@hotmail.co.uk

Edited by Lisa Warburton
www.isisstockport.co.uk

ISBN 978-1-291-39139-8

Contents

3	Questions and Answers from Author
18	A Brief History of Wythenshawe
33	Wythenshawe Hospital
40	The Wall of Appreciation
42	A Wythenshawe Boy
55	Wythenshawe Park
62	I Love Wythenshawe
68	The Baguley Buddha
72	The Ghost of Wythenshawe Hall
76	Manchester Airport
80	Civic Centre
88	Wythenshawe People
92	Fun at Wythenshawe Park Fair
96	Radio Wythenshawe WFM
99	West Wythenshawe Youth Club

Introduction from the author

Question

What inspired you to write a book about Wythenshawe?

Answer

Well, I bumped into a friend from the past I hadn't seen for a long time, who shall remain nameless because their name isn't the important part to why I wrote this book and they were just slagging off everything about Wythenshawe; the people, the place and everything about it.

Question

How did you react?

Answer

I instantly said "Hey hang on a moment, Wythenshawe is a top place, it's got a lot of really nice people living there, like my family, all my friends and many other people I will probably never know, along with people you just meet everyday who provide you a service, like the shop keeper and staff, doctors, nurses, taxi drivers, bus drivers, I could go on and on but you get the picture".

Question

You mean everyday people as well as friends and family?

Answer

Yes, exactly that.

Question

Go on then Ged, what happened next?

Answer

Well, this person wouldn't have it, they continued to say some really horrible negative things about Wythenshawe and anything good and positive I was giving them back about this place, they weren't bothered to take on board or listen about.

Question

What do you think was the reason for this negative attack of bad attitude on Wythenshawe's population of nearly 75,000 people?

Answer

Well, this person had lived in Wythenshawe for over 30 years of their life and moved away to another town for a few years and when I bumped into them and said "Hi, how are you doing?" they replied, "Oh, I don't like the town I'm living in and I'm looking for another place to live in." So that's when I said, "Why don't you move back to Wythenshawe?" That's when I got the abuse about how bad Wythenshawe was.

Question

Okay, I get it now, how did the conversation on the street go?

Answer

I said, you sound very bitter, angry and definitely wrong about Wythenshawe, I find it insulting, I live there and so do a lot of people I love.

Question

How did this person respond?

Answer

Well, by blaming all life's disappointments on everybody else coming from that place, rather than taking a good look at themselves.

Question

How did you reply to that?

Answer

I said something like, you sound too bitter for me, I hope you have a good day and I turned around and walked far away from them.

Question

So was that the seed, if you like, that inspired you to write the positive side about what you call the wonders of Wythenshawe?

Answer

Yes, yes and yes again, I just got sick and tired of hearing people and the media slagging Wythenshawe off.

Question

Have you fallen out with this person and have you seen them since?

Answer

No, because since my defence of Wythenshawe, they must of took a deep think about what I said and since then I got sent a letter of apology and ironically and funny enough, they've moved back into Wythenshawe and were happy to do so. Look, if you start blaming a place you lived in for the life you had, then in my opinion you're on the wrong road, because a place is just a place.

Question

Are you saying the blame lies within ourselves?

Answer

Often enough yes, a lot of people don't like to hear that, but it's not life's events that change you, it's how you react.

Question

So I know you're a Wythenshawe lad and wrote many books, but at this moment in time you've not made any big money from it, why turn your attention to writing about Wythenshawe?

Answer

To show people, how cool Wythenshawe is, to remind people of the good things that are in Wythenshawe and have come out of Wythenshawe.

It's a fantastic place with great people, yes there are bad sides and stories to it as there is with any place, anywhere, anytime, but I'm not interested in focusing on the negative and blowing it up bigger to make it more important. The positive is greater than the negative.

Question

Some critics may say you're wasting your time on creating this book, because even Wythenshawe people won't read it, never mind outsiders, what's your reply to that?

Answer

That's an insult to Wythenshawe again, as if they don't care, or as if they aren't interested, or as if they don't support one of their own people, I think those kinds of critics don't know or understand Wythenshawe.

Question

I know your goal, should you gain fame and fortune, is to help this community with your time, money and any influence you can bring to others with such powers to speak of, maybe in your writing.

Answer

Yes, I'd so much like to help this wonderful place of Wythenshawe, investing in local community projects and such like that would be a dream come true because this place and its people have given me so much and you should never forget your roots.

Question

So this book of yours called 'The Wonders of Wythenshawe', what does it have inside it?

Answer

Well, there are questions and answers from me and for me. A section of how I came from Ardwick to Wythenshawe and fell in love with the place and people. Then poems about the great experiences and places of Wythenshawe I've known and been touched by.

Question

You've also included a brief but very interesting history about Wythenshawe itself haven't you?

Answer

Yes, I have and it's my hope that I've made it amusing and interesting because a lot of people don't know how Wythenshawe used to be and how it became the place it is now and I think its progress and its history is amazing to discover.

Question

Didn't you learn about that at school when you were in Wythenshawe?

Answer

No, its crazy isn't it, we learned more about Japan or Africa than we did on our own door step, yes of course, learn about other countries but come on, learn about your roots, the place you live in, that's important first I think, then expand out and learn about the rest of the world.

Question

Do you think more people would have respect and love for the place they live in, if they knew and were taught its beginnings?

Answer

Honestly, I think they would, to see how it used to be and it's growing up to what it is today would be awesome, if people only knew how beautiful Wythenshawe was in the 1920's, they would be shocked and go 'wow'. I'm talking about many meadows and fields, woods filled with trees, brooks and streams, cobbled roads, market gardens that fed Manchester fresh tasty vegetables. The innocence, the culture, Wythenshawe was a jewel of a place in the Cheshire countryside and it sacrificed all that and gave it up to save many people from living in Manchester's over crowded city slums.

Question

Do you get upset when people slag off Wythenshawe?

Answer

Yes, but I understand it's coming from a mind of ignorance, they don't know how great this place is, Wythenshawe doesn't commit a crime, it's a person that does. In Wythenshawe, birds still sing, flowers still bloom, trees display their beauty, insects go about their business, the clouds come and go, the rain falls, the sun shines, Wythenshawe is not bad, it's certain people's action that live there that are bad. The amount of good, kind and caring people's actions living there that are great and positive is overwhelming.

Question

It seems to me you really love Wythenshawe and in what you write, both in your poetry and philosophy explains why that is, what then is the intention of this book, to sum it up?

Answer

As a Wythenshawe lad I'm very lucky to have been here and grown up in it and been enriched and so very much helped and supported by it, this book is my way of saying and expressing a very, very big thank you to Wythenshawe. During my life time I've been lucky to visit and go to many places in Europe and countries like Australia, Bali, Canada and many towns and villages in England on holiday or whatever but I will never forget the day I saw Wythenshawe Park and the day I discovered it from the run down urban slums of Ardwick Manchester, we had actually moved in 1968 to beautiful Wythenshawe.

Question

Finally, before the reader continues to venture forward into the book, what would you like to say to them?

Answer

Well, first of all, thank you very much for reading this book and I hope you find knowledge and inspiration from it and a good energy. I've wrote it from passion and enthusiasm, which is the fuel that lights the fires of my heart. Ultimately this book is about Wythenshawe, but say someone was reading it from another town or place and it inspired them to dig deeper into the early roots and development of how their place came to be, that would be a great thing for me to know. Everything changes and landscapes are destined to disappear, in Wythenshawe at the time of writing, the new adventure and thing is the metro-link but in time that too will disappear and give way to something else.

A very dear soul mate of mine used to say when something was very special, it rocks, so with a sincere heart I say, 'Wythenshawe you rock'.

A Brief History of Wythenshawe

If Wythenshawe can be imagined as a vast and large lake of water then see me as one of its sons skimming a flat stone over its surface and if at best it bounces on to live 5 or 6 jumps before it's gone under and disappeared but you saw its show and performance and got entertained by it, then mission accomplished. In this section of the book I'm only skimming over the surface of this great experiment called Wythenshawe. I hope you like it.

Manchester wanted new land to build on and expand, so in 1926 the city council went to the very rich Tatton family, "Look, we're looking for a very big piece of turf to buy from your Cheshire Kingdom, will you sell us this bit?" They said 'Yes', a deal was struck and the land was bought; that piece of turf was Wythenshawe. Really it was only a field to the vast and massive amount of land the Tatton's had managed to get their hands on. Finally in 1931 after all the legal stuff and map changing, Wythenshawe was now a part of Manchester's empire. The building of new homes could begin to take loads of people out of the inner city slums and poverty where early deaths due to diseases from filthy conditions caused by overcrowding existed.

You have to remember in the 1920's and earlier, Manchester city centre was just like a scene out of Charles Dickens novel Oliver Twist; cotton mills spewing out smoke, hard labour, poor run down houses with no bathrooms, or proper heating, no green gardens, little food, a tough hard life, no social services, no national health, poor education, certainly for the large population of working class and unemployed.

So the Manchester council wanted to offer its people a better way to live and be so it bought Wythenshawe. So here's the maths of it; Wythenshawe is near enough eleven square miles in area or for you modern day students,

28km, and was once known as Europe's biggest housing estate, not just in England but Europe's 'wow', that includes: Germany, France, Spain, Portugal, Italy and the rest of the Crewe.

Yes, we know it's got smaller now because a lot of people ended up buying the council houses they lived in but loads didn't. The thing is these new built houses were fresher, newer, cleaner, had gardens and were in a much better environment, the countryside with its fields, meadows, parks, cleaner air and so on, it became affordable to live in this beautiful place called the now famous used expression 'Garden City'.

Now I want the reader to stay with me, don't get bored because this is the history of where you live and you should be proud of it and I'm going to explain it in laymans terms anyway because that's good and more interesting for me as well as you.

If you don't live in Wythenshawe but are interested in this community, then happy to have you on board.

So, what places make up my beloved Wythenshawe, well there's Baguley, Benchill, Peelhall, Newall Green, Woodhouse Park, Moss Nook, Sharston, Northenden, Crossacres and Brownley Green. If any others get added in the meantime or future, welcome! If I've missed any sorry but I don't believe I have. So Wythenshawe has become its own little kingdom.

I want to take the readers into places and faces and experiences I have known in these pockets of time and days I've lived. If it helps you remember yours or say yes I know what you are talking about, believe me that is the reason I wrote this book.

Oh by the way at the time of writing this book, Wythenshawe has a population of 80,000 people.

This section of the book I've wanted to highlight some of the interesting facts about Wythenshawe without going to deep and long into each one. I figure if you want to know more about anything I've touched upon you'll take that in to dig deeper which I would congratulate you for and maybe you could email me and tell me what you've discovered, that would be fab.

The most famous house I know of in Wythenshawe, is that iconic landmark known to us all and easily identified as 'Wythenshawe Hall', it's hundreds of years old, got a lot of history and mystery to it, it was one of the many houses the Tatton's owned. Fair play to the Manchester Corporation, they put the pressure on that clan to part with it and the land in 1926, how and why any one family should own that amount of land I will never understand.

Now we can see how what was once a part of their claimed farmland was going to be turned into the largest housing estate in Europe, about time to. The name Wythenshawe is relatively new and it can be broken down and understood as meaning 'Wythen, which was willow tree and 'Shawe' meaning wood. So the early Saxons saw a deeply covered area of willow woods, now know as Wythenshawe.

The willow tree is a much versatile tree and valued highly for its wood and strength; it produced the Aspirin drug, so useful in medicine and also the cricket bat used in sport, amongst many other different uses as well. That's why it was highly valued by the Saxons way back in history. Funny how a name gets its name isn't it.

If we just look at the drug Aspirin which helps pain and thins the blood allowing easy flow to the heart, this came from the willow tree, that was so native to Wythenshawe as well as other places as well, but none the less grew abundantly here. I imagine that much like a teething ring to ease a baby's teething pain when bit on, ancient humans who had tooth ache stumbled upon the Aspirin in willow by biting down hard on a piece of twig they put against the problem tooth in their mouth and as they cut into the bark the sap juice that was released soaked into the gum or tooth root and dulled the pain. Actually it's an idea and theory I like and who's to say I'm wrong, I've not heard or read that anywhere but I've just imagined that might be so. Anyway Wythenshawe means willow wood.

The three oldest and ancient townships of Baguley, Northenden and a strange place I haven't heard called Northen Etchells joined up in 1931 to become part of Wythenshawe, before that year they weren't. So welcome aboard I say, interesting isn't it, these places we live in and their history and meaning.

Let's look at Manchester airport, a very busy place now for planes to take off from and land on to, departing and arriving from different parts of the world. It used to be called Ringway

Airport when it was a lot smaller and less busier, before that only three farmers fields between Rackhouse Road and Wythenshawe Road were used as an airport.

It's mad to think how anything we see as massive whether it be an airport as big and international as Wythenshawe's own Manchester airport or even Tesco supermarket or Asda started off as a small shop or strip of field. Just like a tiny acorn grows into a giant oak tree.

When people think of Wythenshawe they see many houses, superstores, industrial estates, many different shops, schools, places of business, but when it's massive housing estate began in the 1920's and championed as 'The Garden City', taking people away from city housing slums, it really didn't have a lot in it. This estate was built without shops, or any of the services we take for granted now, there wasn't much work to be had because there wasn't the businesses we have now, you got to remember it was all mostly farmland, fields and meadows, this place once so isolated and rural had never known such an invasion of people before.

The Manchester council weren't moving people into an area of thriving business and enterprise, it had nothing like that, why would it, this was a land of farms and meadows but hey, let's not look at this as if it's a fault, because it's strength was it was at last an escape from the terrible conditions of the slums and all that went in with it.

In a way it was a promised land of better ways to live. People got their supplies from the then known and established village of Northenden, which by the way was a Saxon name for a place they stayed and lived in, which they called their Northern Den. I think that's cool, don't you?

Anyway in the early days of 1920's migration from the city slums, mobile shops came around to you, a bit like the ice cream van would, only they were selling food and goods you needed to live an everyday life with.

Eventually even if it was slow and not an overnight thing, residents and locals got together and created small shops, small places of work to provide a need and Wythenshawe grew and grew.

Industrial estates like Sharston, Moss Nook and Roundthorn appeared and grew up followed by schools, pubs and churches. It was a fantastic advance of progress taking place and a blue print of success for the rest of Europe's following council estates to take note, Wythenshawe was I think a leader or trend setter in this.

Wythenshawe Hospital is massive now and world famous for its heart and burns units and other good work it continues to do and very few people from Wythenshawe can't say they haven't been grateful to that great place, and yet it all started from a small hospital, it was then known as Baguley Hospital.

I hope the reader understands in this section of my book I am scratching over the surface of how, why and when Wythenshawe as we now know it came about. As you discover in this book I've got my introduction and reasons for writing it, personal poems dedicated to people and places I've met and seen in Wythenshawe and other features it's my intention you will enjoy. Okay now such a growing community needed a central capital to go to for food, entertainment and other vital things, so a big welcome now to civic centre. It has a top class library now full of books, DVD films, courses of education and help.

I can highly recommend it to anyone; it's set in the forum complex which is really a great community centre that has a good gym, swimming pool, leisure facilities, shops, career advice, workshops, medical centre, great radio station, Wythenshawe FM, the Wythenshawe forum is a top, top place.

There are now great housing associations like Willow Park in Benchill and Parkway Green in Baguley that do a great job looking after local council housing for its residents. Remember all this came from farmers fields not really that long ago.

Guess who's writing this book? Yes, that's right, one of the lucky people who have benefitted from the Wythenshawe plan, to get people out of the poor housing and Manchester slums that were doomed to be knocked down.

I was born in 1960 and lived in those Ardwick Manchester slums for 8 years, then in 1968 moved to Wythenshawe's Garden City. Wow, it was love at first sight and I will always be grateful so much to Wythenshawe.

Think of this; Wythenshawe has 12 parks, 18 woodland areas including, I think the Jewel in Manchester's crown of nature and not just

Wythenshawe's treasure, yes I am talking about and praising highly Wythenshawe Park, which covers 270 acres of beautiful green space and is the home to Manchester's only community farm. First how cool is that? It's such a fantastic place, I love it so much and I know so many others do, in fact no one on this planet dislikes it. I won't go further with my admiration of this great place because I praise it in a poem I have written in this book. Other parks include Hollyhedge Park, Peelhall Park, Baguley Park, Northendens Riverside Park. Remember this type of stuff was the stuff of dreams to those of us who left the city slums for Wythenshawe.

Wythenshawe is near enough; 8 miles away from Manchester Piccadilly Centre and its Southern most districts within that great Manchester towns boundary. As I prepare to leave this interesting section of this book, 'The Wonders of Wythenshawe'. I hope I've kept the history of it simple, yet interesting, that's the way I like it and if you want to know more about its history, geographically or politically you only have to go on a computer or write your own book about it. Wythenshawe has produced great things and will go on to do so; I have no doubt about that. It truly is a wonderful place!

Wythenshawe has filmed the highly acclaimed channel four series 'Shameless', but needless to say we're all not like that, but we are humorous in a positive way. There's about 43,000 people who have jobs paid, a lot who have jobs unpaid, let me include the dads and mums and carers in this worthy bracket after the kids they work so hard as well with little or no financial rewards it's done out of love.

Wythenshawe has produced well known institutions of work. Wythenshawe Hospital (previously known as Baguley Hospital), Wylex-Works – a producer of electrical goods, Vimto on Roundthorn estate, a world renown soft herbal drink, Timpsons shoes factory, Manchester's College of the knowledge, Virgin

Media on Southmoor Road and Tesco Supermarket, lately Aldi as well and let's not forget all the corner shops who offer brilliant services to the people. I also include the bus services, ice cream vans, taxi drivers, churches, community project and nursing homes.

Once upon a time Wythenshawe never had any of these services, so from me on behalf of you a big thank you to them all and any others I've missed out like postmen, milkmen and women as well. Soon the metro-link will add to the infra-structure. It used to be said all the roads lead to Rome, maybe now we can say with confidence and why not, all roads lead to Wythenshawe.

Wythenshawe Hospital

Verse One

Now please let me tell you all of this truth,

It's as real as a house that needs a roof.

This is one of England's finest hospitals it should be said,

Whether you visit as an out-patient or get treatment in its bed.

When the sick and wounded arrive through its doors,

'We're here to give the best help', is one of its golden laws.

Working with Mother Nature this hospital is so green,

Growing crops and honey bees it's such a tasty dream.

Verse Two

Now the human body can suffer from its head to toe,

That's why Wythenshawe Hospital is such a reassuring place to go.

When cuts and bruises and broken bones,

Make you sing out painfully those unwanted groans.

The doctors and the nurses will come to your aid,

Now aren't you so glad Wythenshawe Hospital was made?

They've got a hawk that chases pigeons away like a sheriff guards a town,

After all nobody wants those creatures raining their waste down.

Verse Three

How many beautiful babies have arrived on planet earth?

Welcomed by Wythenshawe's Maternity Hospital on their birth.

It's a fact of life we all leave this earth to die,

But Wythenshawe's good at helping the bereaved ones cope to get by.

How many lives have been saved to continue and carry on?

I'm sure each day there's a story about another one.

So appreciation and praise is what this whole poems about,

That's why Wythenshawe hospital deserves a big world shout.

Verse Four

The Doctors and nurses, the porters and all,

There just a few of the many that get a big thank you call.

The cleaners and cooks and the rescue ambulance crew,

Oh what a fantastic job all together they do.

The surgeons and their specials battle to mend and repair,

Three cheers for the volunteers everyone's glad they are there.

Millions of people must have visited this amazing place,

I'm sure it's seen your unique face.

Verse Five

The hospital wards and corridors that lead to care and hope,

Without those staff I call angels how would the patients cope?

A leader of transplants in both lung and a new heart,

Not forgetting the other treatments where do I begin to start?

So people of this good world I'm so proud to say,

Wythenshawe Hospital rocks and is cool in every way.

Verse Six

It shines like a lighthouse in a dark and stormy sea,

Especially when we're feeling lost in the traumas of pains misery.

Sometimes we take for granted the treasures at our door,

A lot of countries haven't got such a wealth for sure.

Now I'm going to take this pleasure in repeating my message twice,

Because I really believe it's true and sounds so nice.

What makes Wythenshawe Hospital great?

It's the whole banquet of care and staff upon its plate.

What makes Wythenshawe Hospital great?

It's the whole banquet of care and staff upon its plate.

The Wall of Appreciation

Verse One

As Wythenshawe Hospitals poet in residence,

It's my intention to capture the evidence.

In the rhyme and reason of it all,

I love the appreciation on the wall.

Written by those in a state of gratitude,

Puts the reader in a happier mood.

I urge all staff to stop and think,

Consume these words like food and drink.

Verse Two

The jobs you do are special and unique,

Every single day of the week.

I'll tell you now and this much is true,

What makes this hospital great is the work you do.

A patient can feel better by your kindness and a smile,

It really makes a difference when you go that extra mile.

So the writing on the wall is from someone's grateful soul,

Always there to remind how special is your role.

A Wythenshawe Boy

Verse One

I came from Ardwick slums to the promised land of Wythenshawe Garden City,

I never did well in the Government schools so I messed about and was witty.

I learned my wisdom from the concrete streets,

Climbing trees and jumping streams were childhood treats.

I was into football and being an angel with a dirty face,

I left Ardwick in 1968 and discovered a much cleaner place.

Verse Two

I was an artful dodger sort of kid,

I could roll a marble down the tightest grid.

Playing with creepy crawlies was lots of fun,

Chasing earwigs and beetles on the run.

Manky rats and cockroaches in Ardwick were common sights,

As an eight year old kid they didn't scare me into frights.

They were just a part of the wildlife scene,

In a place now gone and long past been.

Verse Three

Those crumbling old houses condemned to be demolished and dead,

Were the haunted houses in my fair ground head?

As me and my mates ran up and down the creaking stairs,

Playing batman and robin without no worries or cares.

Exploring the ghost of a wrecked out car,

To us that was Disney land on that burnt old scar.

Having magical fun pretending we were driving,

Dancing on its roofs like we were jiving.

Verse Four

Staring and being hypnotised as a bulldozer eats a building away,

The sound was like a bomb exploding through the day.

As yesterdays children we dripped enthusiasm like sap from a rubber tree,

When we played cowboys and Indians an old blanket was turned into a tepee.

Back then when mobile phones and computers weren't even in a dream,

The latest technology for kids was a plank that bridged a stream.

Verse Five

Yes, I'm rapping about when I was a boy in 1960 and the seventies too,

When you only got new shoes after the holes started coming through.

Stung by nettles and chased by wasps was an annual summer thing,

As was throwing your action man about and sliding it down a string.

Those golden days when a sticky penny chew would rot your teeth away,

Now it costs a fortune to let the dentist have his day.

Verse Six

We feasted on jam butties and crisps where you had to find the salt,

Honest to god, it was in blue wrapping paper and it made you stop and halt.

Those memories still live on in the world of my childhood,

You didn't know what rich or poor was as you rolled around in mud.

Like I say, a burnt old car was a kid's playground,

We'd swarm over it like locusts if one was found.

Verse Seven

Happy days when chimney smoke met and married the fog,

Giving birth to the darkest pea soupers known as blinding smog.

Kids really loved it and played a game called hide and seek,

Our mums and dads cursed it but we wanted it to stay for a week.

Looking back on those times from now, some might say that was poverty,

But if you had a good imagination it was your Aladdin's lamp to rub and find the novelty.

Verse Eight

As you grow old and like a dry reservoir recede from yesterday,

Nostalgia turns into Willy Wonker's golden ticket to see life's a play.

I can never forget old bits of wood and pram wheels making a go-kart,

Then being pushed down some hilly street for a faster start.

Even the wood worm sticking out would need a helmet to wear,

But when you're a kid back then you knew no fear.

Verse Nine

The philosophy from this is true, wealth is found inside,

Where ever you are, make the best of it and enjoy the ride.

Okay, what does that mean and what are my childhood memories saying?

When I came from Ardwick to Wythenshawe I found a better place for playing.

It was the greenest place I'd ever known,

I've been so lucky to live there and call it my home.

Verse Ten

To date I've lived here for 35 amazing years,

I've known bad times where I've watered the ground with tears.

But there's been more laughter and happy smiles,

As I've travelled across Wythenshawe's many miles.

Where ever you go and live in life you'll see villains and clowns,

Ride life's roller coaster and experience its ups and downs.

Verse Eleven

So when I came to Wythenshawe it was my pleasure,

To open its box and dive into its treasure.

Fantastic friends I've had the joy to know,

Places I've loved to be in and go.

I've learned a lot in this great place,

It's where I tied my first shoe lace.

Verse Twelve

Kissed the lips of a girl first time,

Found the magic of verse and rhyme.

Got a hat trick for my school team,

Had my first coffee with cake and cream.

Met the mother of my daughter Jess,

Being a father is the best, Oh yes!

Learned to read and write,

Party through the day and night.

Verse Thirteen

Met my best mates for sure,

Without them I'd be poor.

So what I'm proud to say,

Is Wythenshawe will always stay.

Deep in the very heart of me,

It's in my blood and history.

That's why this book is here to praise,

This beautiful place in so many ways.

Wythenshawe Park

Verse One

Oh Wythenshawe Park, you're full of wonderful things,

More than slides and roundabouts with happy kids on swings.

Such a precious jewel worn upon Manchester's dazzling crown,

All the magic of nature is immortalised on your gown.

How many lucky people have enjoyed the pleasure?

Collecting memories and experiences of your treasure.

Climbing trees and running about and playing bat and ball,

These are just a few of the things as a child I can recall.

Verse Two

Playing hide and seek among the cover of different trees,

Chasing catfish and butterflies with thick mud on my knees.

Laughing as I circled around the steps of Cromwell's statue,

Jumping from the top of them because your mates dared you to.

Hot summer day picnics with jam butties and lemonade,

Ice cream cornets melting as you jumped and fell and played.

Verse Three

Stinging nettles and dot leaf rubs and a paddle in the pool,

That was just a given in the holidays of school.

Oh Wythenshawe Park you're such a happy playground,

Food for the dreamers' imagination to feast on sight or sound.

There's an animal farm with cows and sheep,

Baby piglets cuddling up under the heat of sleep.

Verse Four

There are tennis courts where you can hit an ace,

I tried it once but the balls still lost in space.

Check out the miniature golf course, the best that Manchester's got,

I've been around the world and this is the best of the lot.

You got to check out the greenhouses where different cactus grow,

Honestly it's amazing to see plants from countries you might never go.

Verse Five

In today's world of buildings, growing traffic and noisy places,

Wythenshawe Park is one of nature's relaxing spaces.

It's a heaven on this rock called planet earth,

Because it's always there we neglect its worth.

Verse Six

It's got 270 acres of nature's sweet creation,

More beautiful than Buckingham Palace or any space station.

It's got a mixture of trees and birds and flowers as well,

Wythenshawe Park is a piece of heaven in a world of concrete hell.

Verse Seven

On Wythenshawe Park,

It's easy to praise you.

Time and time again,

For all the things that are true.

Children who grow into parents take their children here,

Through the sunshine, rain and snow and every season of the year.

The Easter fair and fireworks lit on a bonfire night,

Are the things that marvel and capture our sight?

So next time you wander through this park,

Remember to appreciate this famous landmark.

I Love Wythenshawe

Verse One

I love Wythenshawe because it's a great place to me,

I've heard some say it's horrible but I'll never agree.

The memories I've enjoyed and discovered there,

I couldn't have found and lived in any other where.

Wythenshawe Park for instance is a lovely place,

Its make-up always paints a smile on my face.

Verse Two

I love Wythenshawe, oh yes I do,

It's given me a lot so I'd like to say thank you.

Lots of great friends and special memories I've known,

That's why dear Wythenshawe lives in my heart's home.

Yes there's been laughter, fun, sorrow and tears,

But those are the seasons of growth that bring fruits to the years.

Verse Three

I love Wythenshawe because it's in my blood,

Yes the so called bad times and the good.

It's like a stage I've lived a life upon,

I always miss it when I've left and gone.

Most of the time the skies above are grey,

But the playgrounds of Wythenshawe have always brightened my day.

Verse Four

I love Wythenshawe and I'll never forget,

All of its treasures I've discovered and met like climbing trees, jumping across streams and scoring a goal,

It's just a part of my jigsaw that makes a picture whole.

I've been lucky to meet some of life's greatest people here,

Their kindness and generosity has been so precious and dear.

Verse Five

I love Wythenshawe because it's been good to me,

When I arrived from Ardwick slums it was a lovely sight to see.

That was 1968 when I was only eight years old,

Wythenshawe was Manchester's Garden City of nature's gift of gold.

Verse Six

I love Wythenshawe because I have seen,

How rough and bad other places have been.

I think its people have great humour and wit,

There's a great wisdom that says make the best of it.

So my appreciation and respect is true,

When I say with an honest heart; Wythenshawe I love you.

The Baguley Buddha

Verse One

They call him the Baguley Buddha,

More poetry than milk from an udder.

He's a Wythenshawe lad that raps in rhyme,

Faster than a spider spinning a line.

He walks with a hoody and a rucksack on,

He's got no hair cos it's all gone.

Always looking for something to write,

Man, his stuff is far out of sight.

Verse Two

They call him the Baguley Buddha,

His wisdom makes an iceberg shudder.

He wishes every soldier fired flowers from a gun,

That all wars stopped and there never was one.

He's nobody's puppet on a string that's long,

So just be yourself and sing your song.

Verse Three

They call him the Baguley Buddha,

He's done what's badder and gooder.

His pen is a gun that's full of ink,

Just shooting out bullets to make you think.

Imagination is the favourite smile of a clown,

That loves the beautiful face of Wythenshawe's town.

Verse Four

They call him the Baguley Buddha,

That sails through his life without a rudder.

From Royal Oak to Benchill and the Brookland estates,

He's collected memories with a load of top mates.

Rode on the waves of war and peace,

Been praised by some and chased by police.

There's one thing that has grown for sure,

His deep love and respect of Wythenshawe.

The Ghost of Wythenshawe Hall

Verse One

There's a ghost in Wythenshawe Parks great hall,

When I was visiting I heard its haunting call.

I found it sad and such a terrible shame,

The way this females death had came.

Now some had said it was a broken heart,

Others claimed from the execution of a pistols start.

So who's this ghost? I hear you say,

Well it's Mary Webb from history's yesterday.

She was a Wythenshawe girl who lived in this hall,

Brought up by the rich Tatton's to be their servant on call.

Now between November 1643 and February 1644,

This house was under attack and siege by Cromwell's civil war.

The battle was fierce and mighty as deadly killings took place,

In the beauty of Wythenshawe Park we now walk in peace and grace.

So let's go back in time and peep through the curtains of history,

To try and see a chink of light through the fog of this dark mystery.

Verse Two

Now one of the soldiers brought in to defend this house,

Was the sweet heart of Mary Webb her future intended spouse?

But her intended fiancés life soon ended and expired,

As Captain Adams troops took aim, shot and fired.

In the air of surrender when Cromwell's Captain sat on a wall,

Mary silently crept up and shot him dead to fall.

That fateful day was Sunday and February the date,

She was such a gentle girl and not the kind to hate.

Now, by some she was applauded but blamed by all the rest,

We can only presume and guess,

Her fate was not the best.

This ghost I heard a wailing from the corridors of Wythenshawe Hall,

I believe was Mary Webb,

Whispering out her call.

So gentle in its sadness as it reached my ears,

Saying 'revenge isn't comforting when I still cry tears'.

I couldn't help remind her she's a Wythenshawe girl that rocks,

You could hear her laughter vibrate as it chimed to life old clocks.

Manchester Airport

Verse One

It used to be called Ringway a very long time ago,

Now it's Manchester Airport putting on a busy show.

It's a gateway to many holidays, businesses and dreams,

As the planes take off high to sail on fast jet streams.

Waiting on the parking bay sits a giant metal bird,

You step inside its belly once the engine sounds are heard.

It's like a small town once you're in the place,

People coming and going different cultures of every race.

Watch your cases swallowed up as you check them in,

Heading to be scanned is where their journey does begin.

Thousands of staff do many types of jobs here,

They're keeping the airport open every day of every year.

Verse Two

One of the world's best airports and it lives in Wythenshawe,

Bringing money to the area without which we'd be much poor.

Hotels, taxis, different jobs, this is what I mean,

Flights that take you far away to places that you dream.

Round and round the carousel looking for your case,

You know someone has found theirs by the smile upon their face.

Manchester Airport has got a lot of shops,

The air hostesses are pretty, in fact I'd say they're tops.

The Captain's in the big bird's mouth, he's taking off quite soon,

It won't be long before the passengers are
closer to the moon.

Roaring down the runway then up like a rocket
in the air,

It's always nice to look out and see
Wythenshawe's green air.

Civic Centre

Verse One

Civic Centre is the capital of Wythenshawe town,

Their buildings aren't pretty and need pulling down.

Yes the people deserve so much better they do,

Come on the city council build them something new.

Now let's take a look at what Civic Centres got,

As I sharpen my focus on the nice things cooking in the pot.

There's so many good flavours going on here,

The Forum is such a great place that much is clear.

It's got a good gym where fitness and muscles can grow and improve,

The staffs are nice and friendly and they help it run smooth.

Verse Two

There's a decent size theatre that puts brilliant shows on,

It's well worth a visit with the family so go and see one.

There's a safe swimming pool where you can have a great splash,

If you're feeling hungry there's a cafe giving tasty value for cash.

Now check out the library because it's got all that you need,

Like computers, DVD's and not forgetting top books to read.

Lots of different courses for learners, so get out of your bed,

Let the knowledge from the Forum Library entertain your head.

There's also a clinic that will check out your health,

A reception room that helps you get a job to increase your prospects and wealth.

Verse Three

Hey, Wythenshawe Radio shouts out air waves from here,

Broadcasting a mixed bag of stations entertaining and clear.

There's just no doubt about it Civics' Forum is great,

Thanks to all the staff that make it a cool place to relate.

Okay, let's take a look at the shops outside in Central Square,

There are many hidden delights I'm sure you'll find there.

Yes, like I said, those pre-fab building are so seventies dated,

There like Cinderella's ugly sisters with faces concreted and plated.

But there are a whole lot of colourful characters walking about,

Going into shops chatting and then coming back out.

Verse Four

There are girls with tattoos on their necks and false things everywhere,

Lads rolling up backy and smoking the clouds of time in the air.

You can get a whole lot of cheap and cheerful things to buy,

If you like people watching there's much soap opera to spy.

There's a local indoor market that's doing okay,

I think it's all very good I just have to say.

They sell fresh and healthy produce with a friendly face,

So forget the giant supermarkets and get down to this place.

You know what you're getting and that's a good thing,

Whether it be a proper cow pie or a big chicken wing.

There's nowhere like Civic Centre and I will tell you this for sure,

It's well worth a day out for you to enjoy and explore.

Wythenshawe People

Verse One

Wythenshawe people are the salt of the earth,

This poem is a tribute to their worth.

They've got good characters and flavour,

Kind heart and great humour to savour.

You know the one's I'm talking about,

Not the ones who contribute nought.

Verse Two

I don't want to waste my time,

On those who hurt with crime.

The people I'm talking about,

When you meet them there's no doubt.

They're just so nice to meet,

Positive in the way they greet.

Verse Three

They shine out as happy and glad,

Even when times have made them sad.

Always helping where they can,

Even if it disrupts their plan.

These Wythenshawe people are the salt of the earth,

Improving the taste of life just by their worth.

Verse Four

They're the inspiration of this place,

The real beauty on this towns face.

In every street there's more than one,

We should value them before they're gone.

They just go about the day,

Helping others without any pay.

I've seen these people in Wythenshawe.

They make a millionaire look poor.

Fun at Wythenshawe Park Fair

Verse One

The sights and sounds of the Easter fair,

Weave hypnotic magic through the air.

Reminding the old of when they were young,

'I want to go on that' is a song they sung.

There are lots of different rides to thrill and scare,

Many prizes to be won and share.

Try hook-a-duck to win a gold fish,

Or a cuddly toy if that's your wish.

Take your pick and pay the cost,

If there's nothing ventured there's nothing lost.

The smell of candy floss sets the mood,

A tray of chips is walking food.

Verse Two

Disco music fills the ears so loud,

To entertain the fairgrounds crowd.

Twisting around on the waltzers chair,

My head goes dizzy and is lost somewhere.

All these rides catch the eye,

Pleading choose me to the passerby.

Welcome to the haunted house,

That's even scary for a mouse.

The roller coaster goes up and down,

Making some go green and frown.

Mini jets fly around and fast,

As bubbles from a machine go floating past.

Verse Three

The fairground at night is a special place,

Where all the coloured lights illuminate dark space.

The happy caterpillar crawls smiling round its track,

It says to the kids I hope you'll come back.

When you fancy a good bump it's the dodger cars,

Where I've had the wind knocked out of me and seen the stars.

So roll up, roll up and visit this Easter fair,

There's lots of entertainment for everyone there.

The music booms out nostalgically its trance like beat,

As the rides go faster to turn up the heat.

Board a rocket on a mission to Mars,

What kid hasn't circled in different cars?

The great memories I have of Wythenshawe Parks Fair,

Will always live on in this poem I share.

Radio Wythenshawe WFM

Verse One

In the house for Radio Wythenshawe WFM,

Here's why you've got to appreciate the stations in them.

They work for free to get the message out,

Each D.J. controller is special no doubt.

They volunteer for the love of it all,

As they hit a big six over the wall.

Yes they care for the very heart of Wythenshawe,

Without them we'd be much worse for sure.

They inform us of what's taking place,

As their signals ride through the air of space.

Reaching our ears to have its say,

They're helping Wythenshawe in a big way.

Verse Two

They've got interests in fashion and local news,

Also music and debates about different views.

It's nice to know you've got the choice,

Listening to Radio Wythenshawe voice.

As their signals travel on the surfing waves of space,

They champion in sound this great Northern race.

There's something for each and everyone to find,

In Radio Wythenshawe WFM's brilliant mind.

One thing I do know for sure,

This is such a friendly visitor to your door.

So let it in I have to say,

Because Wythenshawe WFM rocks in every way.

West Wythenshawe Youth Club

Verse One

This was a place of fun and games,

Where you could live out your hopes and aims.

West Wythy Youth Club was a beacon of light,

In my memories eye it's still a happy sight.

Music from the juke box and a disco D,J, too,

Meeting all your mates there and planning something new.

Verse Two

There's been romance, laughter, fights and tears,

It's seen it all throughout the years.

Table tennis and throwing darts,

Girls that try to break the boys' hearts.

Jackie Fearan ran the boxing school,

He trained us hard the sweat would pool.

Verse Three

West Wythy Youth Club offered lots of things to do,

Before mobile phones and face book arrived as something new.

Lots of characters you would see in there,

Rhino, Butch and Macca I swear.

Too many guys to give a mention,

But the kind who'd fill out a school detention.

Verse Four

I remember going for a week to the lakes,

On one of the West Wythenshawe holiday breaks.

Ghyll Head Outdoor Centre was the place I stayed,

As me and my mates messed around and played.

Now West Wythenshawe has closed down and gone,

But as a club for me it was number one.

Printed in Great Britain
by Amazon